30 COSE DA FARE DOPO LA PENSIONE

E VIVERE BENE FINO A 100 ANNI

e Oltre...

di Simone Azzurri

Retirees DOC:

30 Things to Do After Retirement and **How to Live up to 100 Years**

Chapter 1: "Welcome to the New Adventure" • Introduction to retirement as a fresh start, not an end. • Exploring common emotions associated with transitioning to retired life. • Practical advice on coping with changes in routine and identity.

Chapter 2: "Exploring Passions and Interests" • Identifying and nurturing hobbies and interests neglected during the working years. • Tips on discovering new passions and interests. • Inspirational stories of individuals who have found joy and fulfillment in pursuing their passions after retirement.

Chapter 3: "Traveling and Exploring the World" • Exploring the benefits of traveling after retirement. • Ideas for adventurous trips, cultural excursions, and relaxing vacations. • Practical advice on planning affordable and memorable trips.

Chapter 4: "Serving and Giving Back to the Community" • Exploring the role of volunteering and service in retired life. • Ideas for meaningful ways to give back to the local community. • Stories of retirees who have found fulfillment in dedicating their time and resources to the needs of others.

Chapter 5: "Self-Care and Active Living" • Discussion on the importance of health and wellness after retirement. • Tips on maintaining an active and healthy lifestyle. • Suggestions for managing leisure time and maintaining a healthy and active mind and body.

Each chapter offers a blend of inspiration, practical advice, and touching stories to help retirees fully embrace this new phase of their lives and live a life rich in meaning and satisfaction.

Chapter 1: Welcome to the New Adventure
Introduction to Retirement: Retirement is a significant moment in every individual's life, marking the transition from decades of work and professional

commitment to a new phase rich in possibilities and opportunities. It is a time when we can look back on our past with gratitude and to our future with hope. While some people may anticipate retirement with excitement and joy, others may feel anxious or uncertain about this change. Regardless of the emotions that may arise, it is important to understand that retirement is a new beginning, not an end. Facing Change: The transition to retirement can be accompanied by a range of emotions, including excitement for regained freedom and uncertainty about what the future may hold. It is normal to feel overwhelmed by this significant change in daily routine. However, it is important to recognize that retirement offers the opportunity to explore new paths and to reinvent oneself. Taking time to adjust to this new phase of life can help reduce the stress and anxiety associated with the transition. Reflecting and Planning: Retirement is also a time to reflect on our past experiences and to plan for the future. We can dedicate time to think about what we have achieved in our careers and the successes we have attained along the way. At the same time, we can examine our values and priorities for the future and set meaningful goals for this new phase of life. For example, we may decide to focus on our health and well-being, explore new interests, or spend more time with family and friends. Embracing Optimism: Despite the challenges we may encounter during retirement, it is important to maintain an optimistic attitude and remain open to possibility. Retirement offers the opportunity to explore new passions, cultivate meaningful relationships, and contribute to our community in meaningful ways. We can choose to see retirement as an exciting new chapter of our lives, full of opportunities for growth and personal fulfillment. Conclusions and Future Perspectives: In conclusion, retirement is a time of transition that may bring with it a range of emotions and challenges. However, it is also a time of opportunity and personal growth. Taking time to reflect on the past, plan for the future, and maintain an optimistic attitude can help us successfully navigate through this new phase of life. Whether it is exploring new interests, spending time with our loved ones, or contributing to our community, retirement can be an opportunity to live a life full of meaning, gratitude, and joy.

Maria, at seventy years old, was a respected and admired figure in the Brooksville community. Her presence was like a beacon of hope and kindness, capable of brightening even the darkest days. Life had taken her through many challenges and tribulations, but she had never lost her faith in humanity and the beauty of life. Born and raised on a small farm in the countryside, Maria learned from a young age the value of hard work and solidarity. Her parents raised her with principles of generosity and compassion, teaching her that true wealth resided in giving to others. When her father died in a work accident, Maria took the reins of the farm, helping her mother keep the family afloat. Despite the hardships, she always found time to lend a hand to those in need, donating her food and time to the community. As she reached adulthood, Maria decided to devote herself entirely to serving others. She worked as a nurse at a local hospital, caring for the sick and needy with kindness and compassion. Her hands were always ready to alleviate pain and bring comfort to those who suffered. After leaving her job at the hospital, Maria dedicated herself to volunteering at the "Light in the Night" homeless shelter. There, she found her true calling: giving hope and comfort to those who felt lost and alone. Every day, she prepared warm and nutritious meals for the shelter residents, putting all her love and care into each dish. But her true gift was her ability to listen and understand. People turned to her for comfort and support, knowing they would find in her a compassionate and wise guide. Maria listened to them attentively and empathetically, offering them words of encouragement and hope. One of the most touching stories of her life was that of a homeless young man named Luca. Arriving at the shelter after losing everything due to drug addiction, Luca was full of anger and despair. But Maria saw beyond his tough exterior and welcomed him with love and compassion. Over time, she managed to instill in him the confidence and hope for a better future. Thanks to her support and guidance, Luca was able to overcome his addictions and find stable employment. Maria's story is just one of many success stories of those who crossed her path. Her kindness and altruism have changed the lives of many people, offering them a new dawn of hope and rebirth. And as the sun rose on the horizon, it brought with it a new day of opportunities and possibilities for those fortunate enough to encounter Maria along their journey.

Chapter 2: Exploring New Passions and Interests

Introduction: Retirement offers the opportunity to explore new passions and interests, opening the door to a world of possibilities that can enrich our lives in unexpected ways. In this chapter, we will examine the importance of discovering and cultivating new passions during retirement and provide practical advice on how to do so meaningfully. Discovering New Passions: One of the most exciting benefits of retirement is the freedom to explore what truly excites us. It's the perfect time to ask ourselves, "What have I always been interested in but never had the time to explore fully?" This question can open us up to a world of possibilities. We might discover a passion for art, music, writing, cooking, gardening, and much more. For example, we could delve into the art of watercolor, experimenting with colors and brushes to create unique works that reflect our creativity and unique view of the world. Reviving Forgotten Passions: Retirement also offers the opportunity to rediscover passions and interests that we may have neglected over the years. We might return to hobbies that once captivated us, such as painting, gardening, or creative writing. For example, if we once loved writing, we could dedicate our time to crafting stories, poems, or memoirs that capture the experiences and emotions of our lives. Exploring New Challenges: Exploring new passions during retirement can also mean challenging ourselves and trying new things. This can be both exciting and daunting, but facing these challenges can lead to significant personal growth. For example, we might decide to learn to play a musical instrument, challenging ourselves with notes and melodies to create music that resonates with our soul and inspires others. Cultivating Shared Passions: Exploring new passions during retirement can also be an opportunity to connect with others and cultivate meaningful relationships. We can join clubs or local groups that share our interests, participate in community events, or simply share our passions with friends and family. For example, if we are passionate about cooking, we could host cooking nights with friends or attend local gastronomic events to discover new recipes and dishes to enjoy and share with others. Supporting Personal Growth: Finally, exploring new passions during retirement can lead to significant personal growth. This may include developing new skills, discovering sides of ourselves that we did not know, and increasing awareness of what truly makes us happy. It is important to take advantage of this opportunity to explore, experiment, and grow as individuals. For example, we might discover a new talent for photography, capturing special moments and breathtaking landscapes that inspire us and fill us with joy. Conclusions: In conclusion, exploring new passions during retirement can be a source of joy, satisfaction, and personal growth. Whether it's discovering new hobbies, reviving forgotten passions, or challenging ourselves with new activities, retirement offers the opportunity to live a life full of meaning and fulfillment. Taking advantage of this opportunity to explore what excites us and cultivate meaningful interests can lead to a more rewarding and satisfying life in our golden years.

As Maria's story continues to illuminate the lives of those who cross her path, there are other stories of generosity and altruism that deserve to be told. One of these stories is that of Roberto, a young entrepreneur who decided to make giving to others the center of his life. Roberto had grown up in a wealthy family, but despite having everything at his disposal, he felt that something was missing in his life. While financial success smiled upon him, he felt a void in his heart that no amount of money could fill. It was during a trip to a developing country that Roberto had an epiphany. During his visit, he saw the poverty and suffering that many people had to face every day. He saw children living in terrible conditions, without access to food, clean water, or education. It was at that moment that Roberto realized that his true mission in life was not to accumulate wealth for himself, but to use his fortune to help others. Upon returning home, Roberto decided to dedicate his life to serving others. He founded a charitable foundation that focused on bringing positive change to needy communities around the world. He built schools, water wells, and provided medical assistance to those in need. But his work did not stop at material assistance. An important part of his mission was also to inspire and educate others about the importance of giving. He traveled around the world, giving motivational speeches and encouraging others to put their resources at the service of others. His story of sacrifice and altruism inspired many people to do the same, creating a global movement of solidarity and compassion. One particularly resonant testimony is that of Elena, a young woman who directly benefited from Roberto's help. Growing up in a poor family, Elena had few hopes for the future. But thanks to Roberto's foundation, she had the opportunity to receive a quality education and pursue her dreams. Now, Elena has become a successful doctor, dedicating her life to providing medical care to needy communities around the world. Roberto's story and those he has touched with his altruism are a tangible example of how a single person can make a difference in the world. Through his commitment and generosity, he has left a lasting impact on the lives of many people, demonstrating that true success lies in giving to others.

Chapter 3: Promoting Physical and Mental Well-being Introduction: Retirement represents an ideal time to focus on one's physical and mental well-being. In this chapter, we will explore the importance of adopting a healthy and balanced lifestyle during retirement and provide practical advice on how to promote physical and mental well-being effectively and sustainably. Benefits of Physical Exercise: Regular physical exercise is essential for maintaining health and well-being during retirement. Not only does it help maintain physical fitness and prevent chronic diseases such as diabetes and heart disease, but it can also improve mood, reduce stress, and promote quality sleep. There are many forms of exercise suitable for older adults, including walking, yoga, swimming, gardening, and participating in senior fitness classes. Finding an activity that we enjoy and that fits our lifestyle can make exercise a pleasure rather than a chore. Balanced Diet: A balanced diet is essential for maintaining health and well-being during retirement. Eating a variety of nutritious foods, including fruits, vegetables, whole grains, lean proteins, and healthy fats, can provide our bodies with the nutrients they need to function at their best. It is also important to drink enough water to stay hydrated and avoid excessive sugary and alcoholic beverages. We may also consider consulting a nutritionist for personalized advice on diet and eating habits. Stress Management: Stress can have a significant impact on our health and well-being during retirement. Finding effective ways to manage stress can help improve quality of life and promote greater happiness and satisfaction. Techniques such as meditation, deep breathing, yoga, and art can help reduce stress and anxiety, improve concentration, and promote inner calm. It is also important to practice gratitude and seek support from others when needed. Promoting Mental Health: Mental health is as important as physical health during retirement. Keeping the mind active and engaged can help prevent issues such as depression and anxiety and promote greater emotional well-being. We can do this by participating in activities that mentally stimulate us, such as reading, playing chess, doing crossword puzzles, or attending courses and cultural events. Additionally, maintaining meaningful social relationships and seeking support from friends and family can be a valuable defense against loneliness and isolation. Quality Sleep: Quality sleep is essential for physical and mental well-being during retirement. Sufficient sleep can help improve concentration, memory, and emotional well-being, as well as reduce the risk of chronic diseases. To promote restful sleep, it is important to maintain a regular sleep routine, create a comfortable and relaxing bedroom environment, and adopt relaxation practices before bedtime, such as meditation or taking a warm bath. Disease Prevention: Preventing diseases is essential for maintaining health and well-being during retirement. This may include practices such as undergoing regular medical check-ups, getting vaccinated against preventable diseases, adopting healthy behaviors such as quitting smoking and limiting alcohol consumption, and maintaining good personal hygiene. Additionally, it is important to be aware of early signs of diseases and chronic conditions and consult a doctor immediately if concerning symptoms arise. Maintaining a healthy lifestyle and adopting preventive measures can help reduce the risk of developing diseases and improve quality of life during retirement. Intellectual and Social Activities: Promoting physical and mental health during retirement is not limited to physical exercise and a balanced diet. It is also important to keep the mind active and engaged through intellectual and social activities. Participating in courses, study groups, or cultural activities can help stimulate the mind, promote creativity, and provide opportunities for lifelong learning. Additionally, cultivating meaningful social relationships with friends, family, and community members can improve emotional well-being and reduce the risk of depression and loneliness. Reducing Dependencies: During retirement, it is important to be mindful of dependencies and take steps to reduce their impact on health and well-being. This may include monitoring alcohol consumption, monitoring the use of prescribed medications, and taking measures to quit smoking. Dependencies can have serious consequences for physical and mental health and reduce quality of life during retirement, so it is important to address them seriously and seek the necessary support to overcome them. Health Monitoring: Finally, it is important to regularly monitor one's health during retirement and consult a doctor if there are any concerns or issues. This may include undergoing regular medical exams, monitoring blood pressure, blood sugar, and cholesterol levels, and paying attention to changes in physical and mental well-being. Timely medical intervention can help prevent or manage diseases and promote a better quality of life during retirement. Conclusion: In conclusion, promoting physical and mental well-being during retirement is essential for enjoying a fulfilling and satisfying life. Adopting a healthy and balanced lifestyle, engaging in stimulating physical, mental, and social activities, and regularly monitoring one's health can help prevent diseases, improve quality of life, and ensure active and rewarding aging. Taking advantage of this phase of life to take care of oneself can lead to greater happiness, satisfaction, and personal fulfillment.

Maintaining good physical fitness is essential for enjoying a healthy and active life. In this chapter, we will explore some key parameters for staying fit, focusing on what to eat and what type of physical activity to engage in. Advice - Balanced Diet: A balanced diet is essential for maintaining health and well-being. Here are some detailed suggestions on what to include in your daily diet: Fruits and Vegetables: Make sure to consume at least 5 servings of fruits and vegetables per day. These foods are rich in vitamins, minerals, and antioxidants essential for your body. Opt for a variety of colors to maximize health benefits. Lean Proteins: Proteins are essential for building and repairing muscle tissues. Choose options like chicken, fish, eggs, tofu, and legumes. Limit the consumption of red and processed meats. Complex Carbohydrates: Complex carbohydrates, such as whole grains, brown rice, quinoa, and sweet potatoes, provide sustained energy and are rich in fiber, which promotes digestion and satiety. Healthy Fats: Include sources of healthy fats in your diet, such as avocado, nuts, seeds, and vegetable oils. These fats are important for heart and brain health. Physical Activity Tips: To maintain a strong and healthy body, it is also important to be active. Here are some detailed suggestions on what type of physical activity to engage in: Cardiovascular Exercise: Aim for at least 150 minutes of moderate-intensity cardiovascular activity or 75 minutes of vigorous activity per week. This can include walking, running, swimming, cycling, or dancing. Strength Training: Incorporating strength training two or three times a week is essential for maintaining muscle mass, improving bone density, and increasing metabolism. Use free weights, gym machines, or your body weight to perform exercises like weight lifting, push-ups, lunges, and squats. Stretching and Flexibility: Do not overlook the importance of stretching to improve flexibility and prevent muscle injuries. Dedicate time to stretching exercises after each workout session or engage in activities like yoga or Pilates to improve your flexibility and relax. Adequate Rest: Finally, make sure to give your body time to rest and recover. Sleep is essential for muscle recovery, energy renewal, and mental health. Aim to sleep at least 7-9 hours each night to optimize physical and cognitive recovery. By following these parameters for a balanced diet and a physical activity regimen, you will be on the right track to staying fit and enjoying a life full of health and vitality.

Chapter 4: Exploring New Destinations and Experiences

Introduction: Retirement offers the opportunity to explore the world and live new adventures. In this chapter, we will examine the importance of traveling during retirement and provide practical tips on how to plan and enjoy unforgettable trips in this phase of life.

Benefits of Traveling: Traveling during retirement offers a variety of benefits for physical, mental, and emotional health. Exploring new destinations and cultures can stimulate the mind, promote creativity, and improve memory and cognitive functions. Additionally, traveling can reduce stress, improve mood, and promote greater satisfaction in life. Exploring the world can also help promote emotional well-being and interpersonal relationships, offering the opportunity to connect with new people and share unique experiences.

Trip Planning: Planning a trip during retirement requires some attention and preparation, but it can be incredibly rewarding. The first thing to do is to decide on the destination based on your interests, budget, and personal preferences. You can choose to explore exotic and distant destinations, take a tour of your region or country, or simply spend time in a place that inspires and relaxes you. Once you've chosen the destination, it's important to plan the details of the trip, including transportation, accommodation, activities, and events to participate in.

Exploring Exotic Destinations: Traveling during retirement offers the opportunity to explore exotic and distant destinations that you may have always dreamed of visiting. You can opt for an adventure in Asia, exploring the ancient cities and breathtaking landscapes of Japan, Thailand, or India. Or you can choose to explore the fascinating culture and rich history of Europe, visiting cities like Paris, Rome, or Barcelona. Regardless of the destination chosen, traveling during retirement allows us to immerse ourselves in new cultures, tastes, and experiences that enrich our lives and leave lasting memories.

Tours of Your Region or Country: You don't have to travel far to live memorable adventures during retirement. Exploring your region or country can be just as exciting and rewarding. You can plan a tour of nearby cities, visit museums, historical sites, and national parks, or participate in local events and festivals. This allows you to discover hidden treasures in your own area and appreciate the beauty and diversity of your country.

Group Tours and Cruises: Traveling in groups during retirement can be a fun and socially rewarding experience. There are many organizations and travel agencies that offer group travel packages specially designed for seniors, including guided tours, cruises, and all-inclusive vacations. These trips offer the opportunity to explore new destinations in the company of other like-minded travelers, sharing experiences and creating unforgettable memories together.

Adventure Travel: Traveling during retirement doesn't have to be limited to guided tours or cruises. You can also opt for more adventurous and independent adventures, such as taking a road trip across the country, trekking in the mountains, volunteering abroad, or going on a safari in Africa. These experiences offer the opportunity to explore the world in a more intimate and authentic way, experiencing unique and unforgettable experiences along the way.

Family Travel: Traveling during retirement can also be an opportunity to reconnect with family and share precious experiences together. You can plan family vacations with children, grandchildren, and other loved ones, creating unforgettable memories that will be treasures forever. This allows you to strengthen family ties, share common interests and passions, and spend quality time together.

Exploring New Flavors and Foods: Traveling during retirement offers the opportunity to explore new flavors and foods from around the world. You can taste local traditional dishes, visit food markets and gastronomic festivals, and participate in cooking classes to learn how to prepare authentic dishes from different cultures. This allows you to expand your culinary horizons, discover new flavors, and appreciate the diversity of world cuisine.

Creating Lasting Memories: Finally, traveling during retirement offers the opportunity to create lasting memories that will accompany you for the rest of your life. Memories of past adventures become precious treasures that we can share with others and that fill us with joy and satisfaction. Whether it's a sunset beach walk, a dinner with a panoramic view, or a conversation with a stranger that becomes a friend, every moment spent traveling during retirement is a gift to be appreciated and remembered.

Conclusion: In conclusion, traveling during retirement is a unique opportunity to explore the world, live new experiences, and create unforgettable memories. Whether you're exploring exotic destinations, taking a tour of your region or country, participating in group tours or cruises, or opting for more adventurous and independent adventures, traveling during retirement offers a myriad of possibilities and opportunities. It's a chance to broaden your horizons, enrich your life, and create lasting bonds with others. Whether you're an experienced explorer or a novice in the art of travel, there has never been a better time to embark on an adventure and discover the world. Making the most of this opportunity can lead to a richer, more fulfilling, and meaningful life in our golden years.

Stress Management:

Stress management is a crucial element for overall well-being. In this paragraph, we will explore new approaches and strategies to address stress in everyday life, as well as provide testimonials and practical advice for managing it effectively.

New Strategies for Coping with Stress: Mindfulness and Meditation: Practicing mindfulness and meditation can help you develop greater awareness of the present moment and reduce stress. Dedicate a few minutes each day to meditation, focus on your breath, and let thoughts pass without judgment. Deep Breathing: Learn deep breathing techniques to instantly calm the nervous system and reduce stress. Try diaphragmatic breathing, inhaling slowly through the nose, expanding the diaphragm, and then exhaling slowly through the mouth. Recreational Activities: Find activities that you are passionate about and that allow you to take your mind off daily stress. It could be reading a good book, painting, gardening, or any other activity that relaxes you and brings you joy.

Success Testimonials: Marco, 35 years old: "I have always had a stressful job, but since I started practicing mindfulness regularly, I have noticed a significant improvement in my ability to manage stress. Now I feel calmer and more focused, and I face challenges with greater resilience." Anna, 28 years old: "After introducing meditation into my daily routine, I noticed a remarkable change in my level of stress and anxiety. Now I can remain calm even in the most difficult situations and maintain a more stable emotional balance."

Additional Tips: Regular Exercise: Physical exercise is a great way to reduce stress and improve your mood. Find an activity you enjoy, whether it's walking, running, yoga, or dancing, and do it regularly. Time Management: Organize your time effectively by planning activities and assigning priorities. Learn to say no when necessary and delegate tasks when possible to reduce workload. Social Support: Seek support from friends, family, or a therapist when needed. Talking about your feelings and sharing your concerns with others can relieve stress and offer you new perspectives.

By adopting these new strategies and listening to the testimonials of those who have successfully dealt with stress, you will be able to manage life's challenges with greater resilience and emotional balance.

Chapter 5: Creating a Meaningful Legacy

Introduction: Retirement is not just a transition from working life to retirement life; it's also a time to reflect on the past, evaluate the present, and plan for the future. In this chapter, we will explore the importance of creating a meaningful legacy during retirement and provide practical advice on how to do so in a way that our impact can last for generations to come. Assessing Your Past: Before being able to create a meaningful legacy, it's important to take the time to reflect on your past and assess the experiences, challenges, and achievements that have shaped who you are today. We can do this by writing a memoir, keeping a journal, or simply taking a walk down memory lane. This helps us better understand ourselves, our motivations, and our values, and prepares us to create a legacy that reflects who we are and what we believe in. Identifying Core Values: One of the first steps in creating a meaningful legacy is identifying the core values that guide our actions and decisions. We can do this by reflecting on what truly matters to us in life and what principles we want to pass on to future generations. These values may include compassion, integrity, generosity, resilience, and much more. Identifying our values helps us live in line with our authenticity and create a legacy that reflects our deepest principles and beliefs. Planning for the Future: Creating a meaningful legacy during retirement requires some planning and preparation. We can start by reflecting on what we hope to achieve in the future and how we can contribute to realizing those goals. This may include financial planning, creating a will or estate plan, donating time or resources to charitable causes, or passing on knowledge and skills to future generations. Planning our future helps ensure that our legacy is intentional, meaningful, and enduring. Transmitting Knowledge and Experiences: An important part of creating a meaningful legacy during retirement is transmitting knowledge and experiences to future generations. We can do this by narrating our life stories, sharing memories and lessons learned, and teaching practical skills and competencies. This not only allows us to preserve our personal legacy but can also inspire and positively influence others along the way. Supporting Charitable Causes: Creating a meaningful legacy can also mean supporting charitable causes and nonprofit organizations that reflect our values and interests. We can do this by donating time, resources, or expertise to organizations that support causes such as health, education, the environment, human rights, or poverty alleviation. This allows us to make a tangible difference in the world and leave a lasting imprint on the community and society as a whole. Cultivating Meaningful Relationships: Lastly, creating a meaningful legacy during retirement means cultivating meaningful relationships with others and leaving a positive impact on the lives of those around us. We can do this through acts of kindness, emotional support, and authentic, meaningful relationships with friends, family, colleagues, and community members. This allows us to leave a lasting impression on the people we encounter along the way and create a legacy that extends beyond our own lives. Preserving Family Stories: An important part of creating a meaningful legacy is preserving and sharing family stories and traditions. We can do this by narrating our family stories, preserving photographs and historical documents, and sharing memories and anecdotes with future generations. This allows us to keep our family roots alive and pass on cultural and historical heritage to generations to come. Promoting Education and Culture: Creating a meaningful legacy can also mean promoting education and culture by supporting educational and cultural institutions. We can do this through financial donations, volunteering in schools and libraries, or participating in cultural events and programs. This allows us to promote access to education and culture for all and leave a lasting impact in the fields of education and the arts. Supporting Health and Well-being: Another important part of creating a meaningful legacy is supporting the health and well-being of individuals and communities. We can do this by supporting organizations and programs that promote physical and mental health, disease prevention, and access to medical care. This allows us to make a positive difference in the lives of others and leave a lasting impact in the field of public health. Preserving the Environment and Sustainability: Finally, creating a meaningful legacy can mean preserving the environment and promoting sustainability for future generations. We can do this by supporting organizations and initiatives that work for nature conservation, ecosystem protection, and the promotion of sustainable practices. This allows us to preserve the beauty and diversity of our planet for generations to come and leave a lasting impact in the field of environmental conservation. Promoting Equity and Social Justice: Creating a meaningful legacy can also mean promoting equity and social justice by supporting causes and movements that fight against injustice, discrimination, and oppression. We can do this by supporting organizations and initiatives that work for human rights, gender equality, civil rights, and more. This allows us to contribute to building a fairer and more inclusive world for all and leave a lasting impact in the field of social justice. Engaging Future Generations: An important part of creating a meaningful legacy is engaging future generations in the process and work. We can do this by encouraging young people to participate in initiatives and programs that promote social awareness, activism, and positive change. This allows us to inspire and guide future generations toward a better future and leave a lasting impact in the fields of leadership and activism. Promoting Individual Empowerment: Finally, creating a meaningful legacy means promoting individual empowerment and autonomy. We can do this by providing resources, support, and opportunities to those seeking personal growth, professional development, and the realization of their dreams. This allows us to help others realize their potential and live a fulfilling life, leaving a lasting impact in the field of individual empowerment. In conclusion, creating a meaningful legacy during retirement is a unique opportunity to reflect on our past, evaluate our present, and plan our future. Making the most of this phase of life to create a lasting imprint can lead to greater satisfaction, fulfillment, and meaning in our golden years.

Whether it's transmitting knowledge and experiences, supporting charitable causes, or cultivating meaningful relationships with others, each of us has the potential to make a difference in the world and leave a lasting legacy for generations to come.

Retired seniors who have enriched their lives: Maria, 70: After retirement, Maria decided to dedicate herself to volunteering at a homeless shelter in her community. Through her commitment and kindness, she helped many homeless people find comfort and support, giving new meaning to her life after retirement. Giovanni, 68: After a career dedicated to working in a multinational company, Giovanni decided to pursue his passion for painting. He attended art classes and started painting regularly, discovering a hidden talent and a source of joy and personal fulfillment. Carla, 72: Carla started practicing yoga after retirement, aiming to improve her physical and mental health. With consistency and dedication, she made significant progress in flexibility, strength, and inner tranquility, proving that age is never a barrier to well-being. Luigi, 75: After losing his wife, Luigi decided to travel the world, exploring new places and meeting different people. Through these experiences, he found comfort, inspiration, and new perspectives on life, proving that joy and adventure can be found at any age. Elena, 68: Elena embarked on a creative writing course after retirement, realizing her dream of becoming a writer. She published several stories and essays, sharing her life experiences and inspiring others with her creativity and passion for words. Antonio, 70: Antonio began pursuing photography, exploring the world through the lens of his camera. His images captured the beauty of nature, the diversity of cultures, and the essence of life, proving that creativity knows no age limits. Giulia, 72: Giulia started attending cooking classes after retirement, learning new recipes and culinary techniques from different cultures. She now hosts gourmet dinners for family and friends, showing that a passion for food can be a source of joy and sharing even in old age. Franco, 73: Franco decided to take up gardening after retirement, transforming his garden into an oasis of colors and scents. Contact with nature and working with plants gave him serenity and satisfaction, proving that even simple activities can bring great happiness. Anna, 69: Anna started studying a new language after retirement, enrolling in Spanish lessons. Thanks to her commitment and determination, she became fluent in the language and was able to travel to Spain and Latin America, enriching her life with new experiences and friendships. Mario, 71: Mario embraced the spirit of adventure after retirement, participating in mountain hikes and trips to remote locations. The physical challenges and the beauty of nature filled him with energy and gratitude, proving that age is just a number when it comes to pursuing one's dreams. Here is a list of 30 hobbies suitable for seniors to do daily:

1. Gardening: Cultivating flowers, plants, or vegetables can be relaxing and rewarding.

2. Reading: Reading books, newspapers, or magazines on topics of personal interest.

3. Writing: Keeping a personal journal or writing stories, poems, or memoirs.

4. Painting or Drawing: Experimenting with colors and shapes can be an excellent way to express creativity.

5. Music: Listening to favorite music or learning to play a musical instrument.

6. Cooking: Experimenting in the kitchen with new recipes or preparing traditional dishes.

7. Walking: Taking walks outdoors to enjoy nature and keep circulation active.

8. Photography: Taking photos of family, nature, or local events.

9. Crafts: Creating craft items such as jewelry, sculptures, or home decorations.

10. Board Games: Playing board games like chess, checkers, or cards with friends or family.

11. Tai Chi or Yoga: Practicing Tai Chi or yoga exercises to improve balance and flexibility.

12. Storytelling: Sharing life stories with friends or family.

13. Volunteering: Helping the community through volunteer activities at hospitals, libraries, or local associations.

14. Cultural Visits: Visiting museums, art exhibitions, or historical sites to learn something new.

15. Manual Work: Undertaking woodworking projects, DIY, or home repairs.

16. Gentle Exercise: Attending gentle exercise or stretching classes to keep mobility active.

17. Book Clubs: Organizing a book club or participating in reading groups to discuss favorite books and authors.

18. Hanging Gardens: Growing plants or herbs on balconies or terraces.

19. Model Making: Building models of trains, ships, or airplanes.

20. Chess: Improving tactical and strategic skills by playing chess with friends or online.

21. Animal Care: Taking care of pets such as dogs, cats, or fish.

22. Puzzles: Solving puzzles or brainteasers to stimulate the mind.

23. Support Groups: Participating in support groups to share experiences and find mutual support.

24. New Technologies: Learning to use computers, tablets, or smartphones to stay in touch with friends and family and explore new online activities.

25. Art Therapy: Participating in art therapy sessions to express emotions through art.

26. Language Courses: Learning a new language or improving linguistic skills through courses or lessons.

27. Local History: Studying the local history of one's city or region.

28. Guided Meditation: Participating in guided meditation sessions to relax and find serenity.

29. Small DIY Projects: Making creative projects such as scrapbooking, Christmas decorations, or sewing projects.

30. Social Activities: Organizing dinners, gatherings, or social events with friends and family to keep social connections active.

Title: "The Senior's Venture: A Journey into the World of Affiliate Marketing"

Testimonial: The Beginning of a New Adventure

It was a bright spring day when Giovanni, a newly retired 62-year-old senior, found himself sitting in his small apartment. He looked out the window with a mix of excitement and uncertainty. He had worked hard all his life, but now, with a modest monthly pension of only 1000 euros, he wondered how he would manage his daily expenses.

As he sipped his morning coffee, Giovanni surfed the internet in search of ways to supplement his income. He had heard about affiliate marketing, a business model where one promotes products or services from other companies in exchange for commissions on generated sales. Intrigued by this possibility, he decided to delve deeper into the subject.

Discovering the Potential of Affiliate Marketing

As the days went by, Giovanni immersed himself more and more in studying affiliate marketing. He discovered that he could promote a wide range of products, from anti-wrinkle creams to cookbooks, from online courses to gardening equipment. His mind filled with ideas as he envisioned the earning potential that this new world offered him.

After grasping the basic concepts, Giovanni decided to put into practice what he had learned. He created a blog dedicated to gardening, a passion he had cultivated for years. He wrote informative articles on how to grow organic vegetables and how to design the perfect garden. Gradually, his blog began to gain visibility and attract readers interested in his knowledge.

Collaborating with Affiliate Companies

With his blog now established, Giovanni decided to seek out affiliate companies to collaborate with. He contacted several online stores specializing in gardening products and proposed to promote their items on his blog in exchange for a percentage of generated sales. To his surprise, many companies enthusiastically accepted his proposal. In no time, Giovanni became an affiliate of several renowned brands in the gardening sector, thereby gaining access to a wide range of products to promote on his blog.

Growing the Online Business

As weeks passed, Giovanni's blog began to grow exponentially. Thanks to his consistent effort and the quality of his content, he attracted more and more visitors interested in gardening. His product reviews became increasingly popular, and sales commissions started rolling in. Giovanni couldn't believe his luck. What had started as an experiment to supplement his income was turning into a real earning opportunity. Every day, he woke up excited, eager to write new articles and discover new products to promote.

Successes and Challenges of Affiliate Marketing

However, Giovanni's journey was not without challenges. He found himself having to contend with competition from other bloggers in his niche and navigate the complex dynamics of online marketing. Nevertheless, with determination and perseverance, he managed to overcome obstacles and solidify his position in the world of affiliate marketing. Over time, his monthly earnings steadily increased, far surpassing his initial expectations. He even secured a sponsorship deal with a major company in the gardening sector, ensuring a steady stream of income.

Giovanni's Future in Affiliate Marketing

Today, Giovanni looks back with gratitude on the day he decided to embark on his journey into affiliate marketing. There have been challenges along the way, but also great satisfaction and successes. Every day, he wakes up with the awareness that his work not only allows him to earn extra income but also to share his passion for gardening with people around the world.

For Giovanni, affiliate marketing is not just an earning opportunity but also a way to keep his creativity, curiosity, and sense of purpose alive. Looking ahead, he is eager to continue his journey and see where the future will take him in the ever-dynamic world of e-commerce and online marketing.

As you can see, it could not only become a hobby but also an extra income to supplement your pension.

Here's another case of seniors who, after retirement, started working online to match their pension income.

Title: "The Senior's Pen: A Journey into Self-Publishing"

Discovering a New Passion

While most people dreamed of retirement as a time of rest and relaxation, for Maria, aged 67, it was the beginning of a new adventure. Since she was young, she had loved writing, but family duties and full-time work had never allowed her to fully pursue her passion. With retirement behind her and a lifetime of experience, Maria decided to pick up her pen again and bring to life the stories she had held in her heart for so long. She immersed herself completely in her world of fantasy, creating vivid characters and worlds rich in detail. Writing became a source of joy and satisfaction for her, unlike anything she had experienced before.

Debut in Self-Publishing

After completing her first novel, Maria decided to explore the possibilities of self-publishing. She had heard about online platforms like Amazon that allowed authors to publish their books in digital and paperback formats without having to go through the traditional routes of publishing houses. With a bit of uncertainty but also with great determination, Maria uploaded her novel to Amazon and published it as an ebook and paperback. She was excited but also a little nervous about how her work would be received by the public.

Unexpected Success

Weeks passed, and to her surprise, Maria's novel began to receive positive reviews from readers. Her stories had captured the imagination of many people, who appreciated her engaging writing and well-developed characters. Over time, sales of her book began to grow steadily. Maria found herself incredulous at the fact that her passion for writing could also turn into a stable source of income. The money she earned from book sales even began to match her modest pension.

Realizing a Dream

With the success of her first book, Maria didn't stop. She continued to write and publish new stories regularly, exploring a variety of genres and topics. Every new book she put up for sale on Amazon received a warm reception from the public, confirming Maria's talent as a writer. Today, Maria looks back with gratitude on the day she decided to embark on her journey into self-publishing. There have been challenges along the way, but also great satisfaction and successes. Thanks to her passion and commitment, she has managed to realize a dream she had held in her heart all her life. For Maria, writing is not just a way to earn extra income but also a form of personal expression and creative fulfillment. Looking ahead, she is eager to continue her journey as a writer and see where her pen will take her in the future.

As the author's note says, transitioning from a life in motion to a sedentary life is not simple, which is why many people who are approaching retirement age are taking up new online jobs to supplement their pension and to feel always active.

I'm leaving you with a small calendar that you can customize to your liking.

Part 2: **The Secret to Living to 100 Years**

Introduction Welcome to "**The Secret to Living to 100 Years**." In this book, we will explore the fundamental principles for a long, healthy, and fulfilling life. Living to a hundred is not just a matter of fortunate genetics but also depends on the daily choices we make. We will examine the key factors contributing to longevity and provide practical advice on integrating healthy habits into your daily life.

Nutrition and Diet A balanced diet is crucial for long-term health. In this chapter, we will explore the basic principles of a healthy diet and provide tips on creating nutritious and tasty meals. From a variety of fruits and vegetables to moderation in portions and the choice of whole foods, you will learn how to make dietary choices that promote longevity and well-being.

Physical Activity and Movement Regular exercise is essential for maintaining a strong and disease-resistant body. We will examine the multiple benefits of physical activity and provide advice on how to integrate exercise into your daily routine, regardless of age or physical abilities. From walking to yoga, you will discover which activities are most suitable for your lifestyle and how to get the most out of physical activity.

Chapter 4: Stress Management and Mental Well-being Stress and anxiety can have a significant impact on our health and quality of life. In this chapter, we will explore practical strategies for managing stress and promoting mental well-being. From meditation to deep breathing and mindfulness, you will learn effective techniques to reduce stress and improve your emotional and mental health.

Chapter 5: Social Relationships and Social Support Social relationships are a fundamental element for emotional and physical well-being. We will examine the importance of maintaining meaningful connections with others and provide advice on how to cultivate positive relationships in your life. From organizing activities with friends and family to participating in support groups, you will discover how social relationships can contribute to your happiness and longevity.

This is just the beginning of the book **"The Secret to Living to 100 Years."** Each chapter delves into a fundamental aspect for a long and healthy life, offering practical advice and tips for integrating healthy habits into your daily life.

Nutrition and Longevity: The Power of Nutrition

Introduction Nutrition has always been a central theme in discussions about health and longevity. In this chapter, we will delve into the crucial role that nutrition plays in determining our quality of life and longevity. From food choices to the composition of a balanced diet, we will analyze how our eating habits can influence our physical and mental well-being over the years.

The Importance of Diet in Longevity A balanced diet is one of the fundamental pillars for a long and healthy life. But what exactly does "balanced diet" mean? It's not just about eating balanced portions of carbohydrates, proteins, and fats, but also about choosing nutritious foods that provide a wide range of beneficial substances for our bodies.

The Mediterranean Diet: A Model of Longevity

Among the various diets examined by scholars, the Mediterranean diet stands out for its numerous health benefits and longevity. Based mainly on plant foods such as fruits, vegetables, legumes, and whole grains, but also on fish, olive oil, and a moderate amount of red wine, the Mediterranean diet is associated with a reduced risk of heart disease, stroke, diabetes, and even some types of cancer.

Longevity Testimonials Testimonials from famous people who have lived long lives can provide valuable lessons on how a healthy diet can contribute to longevity and well-being. Here are some interesting stories:

1. **Grandma Emma, 102 years old:** "I have always eaten the products of my land, cultivated with my own hands. Fresh vegetables, aromatic herbs, and extra virgin olive oil have been the protagonists of my

diet. Never overdoing it, always with moderation and a lot of gratitude for what nature offers us."

2. **Grandpa Giovanni, 98 years old:** "When I was young, I worked as a farmer. We ate what we grew: tomatoes, eggplants, zucchinis... all fresh and seasonal. And then the homemade bread, what a fragrance! A simple and genuine life, made of authentic foods and a lot of hard work, but also a lot of satisfaction."

3. **Grandma Maria, 104 years old:** "My secret diet? Lots of fish! Growing up on the Mediterranean coast, fish has always been our daily bread. I still remember my father coming back from fishing and preparing the freshly caught fish. Fresh, light, and delicious. That's the secret of my longevity!"

Famous Long-Lived Individuals 4. Kirk Douglas (1916-2020): Actor Kirk Douglas, famous for his iconic roles in Hollywood cinema, lived to the age of 103. His longevity was also attributed to his active lifestyle and healthy diet.

5. **Olivia de Havilland (1916-2020):** Legendary actress Olivia de Havilland, winner of two Oscars, reached the age of 104. She was known for her love of a healthy lifestyle and balanced diet.

6. **Adele Dunlap (1902-2017):** America's oldest woman at the time of her death, Adele Dunlap, lived to the age of 114. Although not a celebrity in the traditional sense, her longevity attracted media attention and inspired many with her lively spirit and zest for life.

These testimonials demonstrate that a healthy and balanced diet can be a key element for a long life full of vitality. Incorporating healthy eating habits into your daily routine can be the first step towards active aging and lasting well-being.

Grandpa Mario, 102 years old: Life as an Unstoppable Symphony

"When I look back on my long life, I see an intricate musical work, full of high and low notes, joyful and poignant melodies. I was born in an era of great changes, but also of great hopes. Mine has been a life lived between the lines of a score written by destiny, yet I have learned that we can influence the tone of our melody with the choices we make every day, especially when it comes to health and well-being. I have been blessed with robust health since childhood, but I learned early on that health is a melody to be carefully composed. Growing up, I saw the world transform before my eyes: I lived through two world wars, witnessed the birth of television and modern technology, experienced love and loss, joy and pain. But at every stage of my journey, I have always sought to maintain a balance between body, mind, and spirit. My diet has been one of the keys to my longevity. Growing up in a farming family, I learned to value fresh, local food. My mother's garden vegetables, the freshly baked bread from the village oven, the homemade cheese... every bite was a tribute to the generosity of the earth and the hard work of farmers. Even in old age, I continued to follow a diet rich in fruits, vegetables, fish, and olive oil, keeping processed foods and sugar-rich foods at bay. But health goes beyond diet. I have always believed in the power of movement and physical activity. Although I never attended gyms or followed rigorous training programs, I have always maintained an active lifestyle. Long walks in the open air, gardening sessions in my small garden, games of bowls with neighborhood friends... every moment spent in motion was an investment in my future well-being. But perhaps the most important secret of my longevity has been keeping alive my passion for life. I have continued to cultivate my interests and relationships, to learn new things and pursue my dreams. Even at 102, I wake up every morning with a sense of gratitude for the day ahead and with the awareness that life is a precious gift to be celebrated every day. Longevity is not just a matter of genetics or luck, but also of conscious choices and a resilient spirit. I am grateful for every note of my long symphony, and I will continue to play my melody with joy and determination as long as my heart beats."

This testimony of Grandpa Mario reminds us that life is a work of art to be carefully composed with care and passion, and that longevity is the result of a healthy lifestyle, meaningful relationships, and a mind open to new experiences.

Testimony of Giulia Rossi, 94 years old: An Inheritance of Wisdom and Vitality

I am Giulia Rossi, and I have had the privilege of living 94 years full of experiences, challenges, and joys. When I reflect on the secret of my longevity and health, one word comes to mind: balance. Since my youth, I have sought to maintain a balance between mind, body, and spirit, and I believe this has significantly contributed to my long and healthy life.

An Active Life Connected to Nature Since childhood, I have spent a lot of time outdoors, enjoying nature and engaging in regular physical activity. Growing up in a small countryside village, I learned the importance of movement, breathing fresh air, and appreciating the beauty that surrounds us. Even now, in my advanced age, I take daily walks in the park near my home and indulge in gardening, which fills me with joy and keeps me active.

A Simple and Nutritious Diet My diet has always been based on simple, natural, and nutritious foods. Growing up in a farming family, I learned to appreciate the products of the land and have always favored fruits, vegetables, whole grains, and legumes. Home cooking has been my faithful companion throughout my life, and even today, I love preparing healthy and tasty dishes with fresh, seasonal ingredients.

Maintaining an Active and Curious Mind An active mind is just as important as a healthy body. Over the years, I have cultivated my mind through reading, writing, and participating in activities that stimulate my creativity and curiosity. I enjoy solving crossword puzzles, writing poetry, and keeping a journal of my thoughts and experiences. Learning new things has always been a pleasure for me: I learned to play the piano at the age of 70 and studied foreign languages in my old age.

Sharing and Love as a Source of Happiness Finally, I believe that a happy and fulfilling life is built on love and sharing. I have been fortunate to have a loving family and trusted friends who have supported me in difficult times and with whom I have shared moments of joy. The ability to love and be loved is what makes life worth living, and I am grateful every day for the wonderful people I have by my side.

In conclusion, I believe that the secret to a long and healthy life lies in the balance between body, mind, and spirit, in love and sharing, and in appreciating every single day as a precious gift.

The Importance of a Balanced Diet

In this chapter, we will explore the importance of a balanced diet for maintaining health and promoting longevity. Through practical advice, testimonials, and reflections, we will seek to understand how our dietary choices can influence our physical and mental well-being.

1. Basics of a Balanced Diet A balanced diet is essential to ensure that our body receives the nutrients it needs to function properly and to prevent chronic diseases. The basic guidelines include:

- Consuming a variety of foods: Include fruits, vegetables, whole grains, lean proteins, and healthy fats in your daily diet to ensure you receive all essential nutrients.

- Limiting the consumption of processed and sugar-rich foods: Minimize the consumption of packaged foods, sugary drinks, and sweets, which can contribute to weight gain and the risk of heart disease and diabetes.

- Drinking plenty of water: Maintaining adequate hydration is crucial for the proper functioning of the body and for promoting overall health.

2. Aphorisms on Diet Aphorisms and proverbs can offer wisdom and inspiration when it comes to diet and healthy lifestyle. Here are some examples:

• "We are what we eat." This ancient saying reminds us that our dietary choices have a direct impact on our health and well-being. • "An apple a day keeps the doctor away." This proverb emphasizes the importance of consuming fruits and vegetables every day to maintain a healthy and disease-resistant body. • "Eat to live, not live to eat." This aphorism invites us to consider food as a source of nourishment and energy, rather than as a source of pleasure or comfort.

3. Success Stories Listening to the experiences of people who have adopted a balanced diet and seen improvements in their health can be motivating and inspiring. Here are some success stories: • Marco, 65 years old: "After adopting a diet rich in fruits, vegetables, and lean proteins, I lost weight, lowered my cholesterol, and improved my energy and vitality. I feel ten years younger!" • Anna, 70 years old: "I've always had digestive issues and abdominal bloating, but since I eliminated dairy and fried foods from my diet, my symptoms have significantly reduced. Eating healthily makes me feel light and full of energy." • Luigi, 75 years old: "I've learned to cook healthy and tasty dishes using fresh and natural ingredients. Now I eat with pleasure and satisfaction, knowing that I'm doing good for my body and mind." These testimonials demonstrate that a balanced diet can lead to tangible results in terms of health and well-being, regardless of age. **4. Conclusions and Reflections** In conclusion, a balanced diet is a fundamental pillar for a healthy and long life. Choosing nutritious and varied foods, drinking plenty of water, and adopting healthy eating habits can make a difference in our health and overall well-being. Aphorisms and success stories remind us of the importance of making conscious choices when it comes to nutrition, to live a life full of vitality and health.

Maintaining Physical Activity for a Long Life In this chapter, we will explore the importance of physical activity in promoting a long and vibrant life. Through practical advice, exercise tips, and success stories, we will seek to understand how adequate physical activity can contribute to our overall well-being. **1. Benefits of Physical Activity** Regular physical activity brings a wide range of benefits for physical and mental health. These include: • Improved heart health: Aerobic exercise, such as walking, running, or swimming, helps strengthen the heart and improve blood circulation, reducing the risk of cardiovascular diseases. • Weight maintenance: Physical activity helps burn excess calories and tone muscles, contributing to weight control and obesity prevention. • Increased strength and balance: Resistance exercises, such as weightlifting or yoga, help strengthen muscles and improve balance, reducing the risk of falls and injuries. • Mental health benefits: Physical activity releases endorphins, brain chemicals that promote well-being and reduce stress, anxiety, and depression. **2. Exercise Tips** To get the most out of physical activity, it's important to adopt a gradual and sustainable approach. Here are some practical tips: • Find an activity you enjoy: Choose a physical activity that you find enjoyable and engaging, whether it's walking, dancing, gardening, or playing a sport. • Set realistic goals: Set achievable and progressive goals for physical activity, considering your current fitness level and individual needs. • Schedule exercise: Dedicate regular time to physical activity, incorporating it into your daily routine to make it a habit. • Variety: Alternate between different types of exercise to engage different parts of the body and prevent boredom or monotony. **4. Conclusions and Reflections** In conclusion, regular physical activity is a fundamental pillar for a long and healthy life. Choosing an activity that we enjoy, setting realistic goals, scheduling exercise, and varying activities are all useful strategies for maintaining adequate physical activity. Success stories demonstrate that it's never too late to start, and that physical activity can lead to significant improvements in health and overall well-being.

Don't Stay Idle One last piece of advice. For someone over sixty, keeping the mind and body active is essential for a satisfying and fulfilling life. Remaining idle can lead to a range of problems, both physical and mental. That's why it's so important to engage in meaningful and stimulating activities even in old age.

1. Mental Stimulation: Keeping the mind active through intellectual and creative activities can help preserve cognitive function and prevent age-related cognitive decline. These activities include: • Reading: Reading books, newspapers, magazines, or even just solving crosswords or puzzles can stimulate the brain and improve cognitive skills. • Strategy Games: Games like chess, bridge, or word games can help keep the mind agile and train memory and concentration. • Learning: Continuing to learn new things, whether it's a new language, a hobby, or a

digital skill, can keep the mind lively and stimulated.
2. Physical Activity: Regular physical exercise is essential for keeping the body healthy and functioning. Even for those over sixty, there are many suitable options: • Walking: Walking outdoors is a great way to keep circulation active, strengthen leg muscles, and enjoy the surrounding nature. • Strength and Flexibility Exercises: Even if you can't engage in high-impact activities, exercises like yoga or tai chi can improve balance, flexibility, and muscle strength. • Recreational Activities: Dancing, swimming, or participating in fitness classes specifically designed for seniors are great ways to stay active and have fun.
3. Socialization: Maintaining strong social ties is crucial for the emotional well-being of those over sixty. Finding opportunities to meet friends, participate in interest groups, or volunteer can help prevent social isolation and depression. **4. Hobbies and Interests:** Cultivating hobbies and interests can bring purpose and joy to life after sixty. Whether it's gardening, painting, cooking, music, or any other passion, dedicating time to what you love can bring great satisfaction. In conclusion, staying mentally,

physically, and socially active is key to healthy and fulfilling aging. While abilities and needs may change with age, there are always ways to continue living a meaningful and fulfilling life.

You Don't Have to Just Survive, But Live Absolutely! It's important not only to survive but also to live fully and appreciate every moment. Living a meaningful and satisfying life requires more than just daily survival. Here are some ways to do it:

1. Cultivate Passions and Interests: Find what you're passionate about and dedicate time to it. Whether it's hobbies, art, music, sports, or anything else, pursuing passions enriches life and brings joy.

2. Explore New Experiences: Be open to new experiences and adventures. Travel to new places, try different foods, meet interesting people. Every experience offers the opportunity to learn and grow.

3. Nurture Meaningful Relationships: Cultivate bonds with friends, family, and community. Meaningful relationships bring joy, emotional support, and a sense of belonging.

4. Live with Gratitude: Practice gratitude for the small things in life. Appreciating what you have helps maintain a positive perspective and overcome challenges.

5. Experience the Beauty of Nature: Spend time outdoors and immerse yourself in the beauty of nature. Observing trees, stars, flowers, and animals can bring peace and serenity.

6. Embrace Personal Growth: Be open to learning, growing, and improving yourself. Read books, take courses, seek new challenges that help you develop your potential.

7. Practice Kindness: Be kind to yourself and others. Acts of kindness, compassion, and altruism can bring joy to both you and others.

8. Live in the Present: Enjoy the present moment rather than worrying about the past or the future. Practice mindfulness and focus your attention on what you're doing right now.

9. Have a Sense of Purpose: Find a sense of purpose and meaning in your life. This could come from helping others, pursuing your passion, or contributing to your community.

10. Laugh and Smile: Don't take yourself too seriously. Laughing, joking, and finding the funny side of situations can relieve stress and bring lightness to life. Living fully requires awareness, gratitude,

courage, and openness. It's a choice you make every day, a commitment to live with fullness and joy, not just exist. I'm sure the book will be of great help to anyone who reads it, offering not only wisdom and practical advice but also inspiration and motivation to live a full and satisfying life. Here are some websites that might be helpful in finding interesting hobbies and extra earning opportunities:

11. Freelancer.com: This site allows you to find freelance projects in various fields, from creative writing to graphic design, administrative work, and more.

12. Upwork.com: Similar to Freelancer, Upwork is a platform that connects freelancers and clients looking for services of various kinds, offering flexible and lucrative job opportunities.

13. Fiverr.com: On Fiverr, you can offer your services in a wide range of categories, such as writing, editing, graphic design, translation, programming, and much more, setting your price and working hours.

14. Amazon Mechanical Turk: This is a micro-tasking site operated by Amazon, where you can complete small tasks online in exchange for payment.

15. TaskRabbit: If you're handy at small home repairs, assembling furniture, running errands, or other similar tasks, TaskRabbit might be an option to find occasional work in your area.

16. Swagbucks: This site allows you to earn money and gift cards by completing online surveys, watching videos, shopping online, and more.

17. UserTesting: If you're familiar with the web and digital devices, you can earn money by testing websites and apps for usability and providing feedback to developers.

18. Medium: If you have a passion for writing, you can publish articles on Medium and earn money through the Medium Partner Program.

19. YouTube: If you have skills or knowledge to share, you can create videos on YouTube and earn money through advertising, sponsorships, and other income sources.

20. Etsy: If you're skilled at creating handmade items, you can sell your creations on Etsy and reach a wide audience of interested buyers. I hope these sites offer you many interesting and

satisfying opportunities! Finally, I'll leave you my personal website if you need an in-depth consultation.

http://www.simoneazzurri.com

http://www.andiamosulpersonale.com

http://www.affiliazionismart.com

Contacts: Whatsapp: +39-393-5995997 Telegram: +39-393-5995997 e-Mail: staff@simoneazzurri.com e-Mail: info@simoneazzurri.com Testimonials: http://www.simoneazzurri.com/testimonials Appointment calendar: https://calendly.com/azzurri-simone/consulenza-simoneazzurri

Good Life

Simone Azzurri